AF365976

Schizo-National Anthems

Paata Shamugia

Translated by
Manana Matiashvili & Kristian Carlsson

→ www.dracopis.com

⇄ beard@dracopis.com

↻ This book is published with the support of the Georgian National Book Center
& the Ministry of Education, Science, Culture and Sport of Georgia

ISBN 978-91-87341-10-6

Dracopis_008
Schizo-National Anthems
First edition. All rights reserved.

BY   Paata Shamugia
&   Translated from Georgian by Manana Matiashvili & Kristian Carlsson
+   "Solution," "Alibi," *I'm writing…*, "A Busy Poet," & "Why Do I Write?"
      translated by Paata Shamugia & Kristian Carlsson
+   "Compromise" & "Trading Places" previously published in *Jacket2*
      translated by Paata Shamugia & Charles Bernstein
+   *I've always wanted…* translated by Paata Shamugia.
¶   Published by Dracopis Press, Malmö, Sweden, 2018
¶   EUROPE: Printed by Lightning Source, UK, 2018
¶   USA: Printed by Lightning Source, USA, 2018
©   2018: The writer & the translators

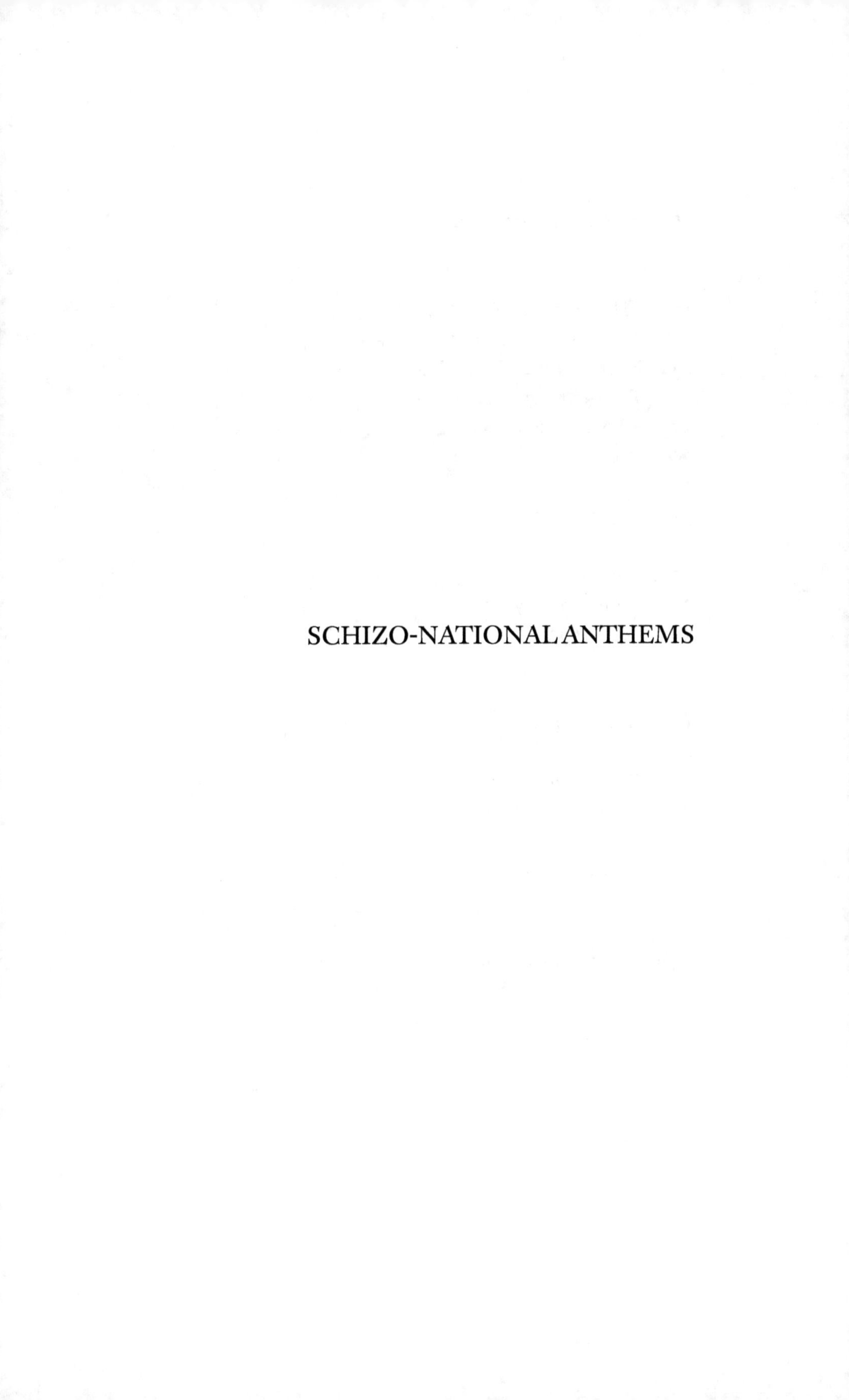

SCHIZO-NATIONAL ANTHEMS

From **Advantage** (2010)

From **Contra Epos** (2006)

Preface: Conversation

1.

Paata Shamugia was born in 1983 and lives in Tbilisi. He is a refugee in his own country and can't return to his home village in Abkhazia—a region still occupied by Russia. Since his father took part in the resistance against Russia during the war in Abkhazia in the early nineties, even Paata is banned from entering the occupied zone—anyhow, his childhood home has been demolished, as well as other houses owned by Georgian combatants from the conflict.

"I have never written about Abkhazia, or about my position as a refugee," he explains. "I don't know why. Maybe because it is to painful. Abkhazia is a highly charged subject for Georgia, particularly in relation to Russia. I know that I always write about myself even when I am writing about other things, as all writers do in all honesty, but I have yet to relate to Abkhazia in my poetry."

"Do you feel any hatred?"

"I would say that almost everyone in this country is a patriot, but I have another way of being that, and for this reason there's a lot of affiliations in Georgia that would consider me being a traitor. But I think we need more equality and democracy—while they believe we need more religion and traditions. I can't picture them aiming for the future. Unfortunately we are in minority in the country, we who think like that, the younger generations included—who has been indoctrinated by their parents. They have become conservative. Their parents are first and foremost afraid of things like sexual liberation, drugs and all experiences they never had themselves."

As a poet Shamugia is tremendously playful, with a tender but distinctive irony throughout his poems. An irony bordering satire, but still considered harmless by a reader from a fully secularized country. As is not the case of Georgia.

"My latest book is titled *Mother Tongue,* which was also the name of the first Georgian textbook for children—written by Jacob Gogebashvili, and published in 1876. That book still plays a major role for Georgians in general—and there are a lot of people who have some kind of religious resistance to any 'abuse' of the classics. Modernists always violate the classics, but in Georgia people take offence and feel hurt by it."

Mother Tongue is the seventh book since his debut in 2006. He has certainly become notorious, but at the same time widely acclaimed, within the establishment as well. Hence I ask him:

"How does it feel to be the first poet to be awarded twice with the national Saba Prize for best poetry collection of the year?"

"The first time I was really nervous—it was with my third book. 'Have I really accomplished something meaningful!?' I asked myself. Meanwhile I felt a lot of tension due to all the surrounding commotion. The following year, when I received the prize for the second time, I was completely calm and thought to myself, 'Okay, this is good.'"

"What is it about your poetry that causes such controversy?"

"The social and political themes. I criticize the traditional opinions of society, and I do it harshly. Conservative newspapers called me both 'bastard' and 'traitor' already when i published my first book of poems—in *Anti Epos* (in Georgia known as *The Anti Tiger's Skin*), I made a parody of the Georgian national epos: *The Knight in the Tiger's Skin* [aka *The Knight in the Panther's Skin*, for English readers] by Shota Rustaveli. I interposed quite a few erotic passages as well, and made a parody of the standpoints of the Orthodox Church. But in my poems 'God' is just a small portion of the dialectical play, and I enjoy having imaginary friends, such as God and other monsters. However, God has no unique position in this case, I write about fishes and birds too."

"Do you feel restrained in your work due to the abusive criticism?"

"No... And thus the conservative media still calls me 'bastard' and 'traitor'. You know, in Georgia we have something called 'The Society of Orthodox Parents'—they bought all copies they could get hold of to prevent my first book to be spread. And burned the books, for real. It was good for me, though—as I then could receive payment for the whole edition, while having the sensation that my writings made an impact. Although it turned into a rather dangerous situation as well, since I got death threats by orthodox extremists."

I made my first interview with Paata Shamugia in Kazbegi, a small village surrounded by beautiful views of the Caucasus Mountain peaks. Little did I know that this region until recently was included in the dissuasion against travel—leaving me, at that time, in a position where I unknowingly had neglected the advice and regulations of my home country. Of course every inch of land was soothingly calm, even the old Military Road onward to the Russian border. The misrepresentation of Georgia seems to indefinitely confuse people; to the point that even officials forget to, in due time, define some specific portions of the country as being safe. Rest asured, now Kazbegi is 'officialy' safe too.

On the other hand Abkhazia has been occupied by Russia for twenty years now. And being back in Georgia, driving the slow highway from Tbilisi to Batumi, alongside the mountain range, there were also the view of villages built for internal refugees from South Ossetia—the second of the occupied regions in Georgia.

Last time, Shamugia asked me to what extent people would care about the specifics of Georgian culture.

"Let them be replaced in my poems, by more common experiences," he said.

And I kind of refused.

This time he reminds me, looking at these "preliminary" villages:

"What do people care about the state of Georgian sovereignty?"

Well, who cares about anything nowadays, outside of their own realms—other than whatever people make a big fuss about? The details are essential. In the details of Shamugia's poems, we find the exiled individual fighting the church, the curruption of the state, the distortion of human decency, the prominent pseudo-evidence against his own rights.

At another passage in between mountains, he suggests the elevated position of some wind turbines could be a nice spot for placing a gargantuan Don Quixote. Any occupation by foreign power, that the surrounding world won't take seriously enough, will surely make citizens feel like Don Quixote. Until having assured themselves that it is the world that has gone mad.

Being "internally displaced" for years, Shamugia doesn't take his literary revenge on Russia. And neither will you find any Soviet kitsch. He is displacing the foundations of Georgian society. Maybe he is a realist. A realist aiming for change. And Russia won't change on his behalf. It is for his own country he is chanting theese Schizo-National Anthems. Holding up a mirror of religion at the brink of self-effacement, sexuality at the brink of humiliation, self-sufficiency at the brink of perversion, and history at the brink of overpoliticization—all in a blur.

Let the injustices be amusing until you can laugh no more.

But despite its appearance, the poetry of Shamugia is no joke.

"As a poet," he says, "I have made many mistakes—but it is my fundamental right, and I make use of it."

Can a poet be wrong?

Can the world be right?

Kristian Carlsson

Mother Tongue

Truisms—to be Learnt by Heart

1.

It's impossible not to be in two different places at the same time.

2.

My absence is limited.
I'm always somewhere even when I'm nowhere.

3.

By conceding that I'm not anywhere,
means I can be everywhere, hence I am God.
If I am God, then why do 300.000 children starve in Georgia?
(It's this year's statistics only),
or, why is it impossible for me to go to Ibiza on holidays?
(This is eternal statistics),
or, why do butterflies die at night
while hypocrites don't?
Agreed. I am not God.
Full stop.

4.

If you exist you must be somewhere,
to be somewhere is to be with somebody,
would be best—if with a lover,
would be worst—if having lunch with the prime minister.

a) My existence is determined by space.
   To some extent, I'm always positioned
   in one definite and awkward point of space.
   And my feet commit an eternal distribution of my body
   from home to work and back again.
   My existence is limited
   as is my non-existence,
   which is already discussed above.
   That's enough.

5.

In Georgian "to be" means "being" and also it means "enough".
The summarize: existence should be enough for us,
though it's not enough for me.
Me being a poet means I look like a slut for whom existence
is a never-ending love.

a) I'm a poet. What do these empty words imply?
   I don't even know what a poet looks like.
   From time to time I try to act as a human being.
   That's all.

6.

A poet must be sexually attractive.
What can be more sexual than a poem?
"A girly girl!" answers Rezo
with a phrase he once heard in a movie.
What can I say? That's hard to refuse.

7.

They say I'm a radical author.
They say I ruin the harmony of verses.
With an elegant gesture, I point to them
where to put their euphonical verses.

8.

When I write I become more than I am,
more than a porridge of the molecules,
more than an incidental blend of fat and proteins.
Maybe this is poetry,
maybe this, this was poetry
from the very beginning
or in the end.
I don't mind.

Literature and Technology

I hurled a great novel by Camilo José Cela
at the night butterfly, smashing it against the wall.
Got it? Step by step literature becomes practical,
while technology tries to somehow take its place:
The iPhone fits the hand better,
seems to have surrendered to the shape of fingers.
Well, let's not behave as ungrateful people,
but Camilo José Cela, we have to confess,
is better at killing butterflies.
Once I used to bring a paperback edition of Lasha Nadareishvili
to the bathroom
but then the super soft toilet paper appeared
(God bless high tech!)
and his books became useless.
That's a pity, but what to do? That's how
technology deals with literature.
I have nothing against my fridge from Bosch—
it freezes better than, say, Camilo José Cela,
but, to be honest, with a book titled *The Family of Pascual Duarte*
you can thoroughly ruin a complete family of butterflies.
Look, this is where its power lies—
in practice, in destruction... Who would expect that!?

I'm looking at the butterfly right now, like a speechless mourner.
It seems to have become the sacrifice of great literature.
I think we might be able to understand each other better now—
me and the butterfly.

The Interrogative Sentence

What to do
with someone whose CV won't fill eight pages
and there's fortune for him to seek in a foreign country?

How does one enter the dreams of a fairy tale prince
being a girl who didn't inherit long legs
in the genetic lottery
and whose only winning ticket
gave a carved nose?
How can she ever find a prince
who will deny all those ideals of beauty
defined by unidentified people?

Where is an eternal loser
going to find an eternal winner—
someone whose CV is as full as the full moon,
whose heart is as sweet as a sweet home,
whose feelings are as tender as tender ferments,
whose love is as solid as solid waste...
How can he restore the balance of the universe?

The balance of the universe did end up on the cross,
but now it is vacant,
who will change Jesus, who will come after him?
Not that one, who has changed the humans?
Who is going to push the third crow out of the rooster's throat?
Who will hang Peter's piercing denials in the air?
Who will lend a hand to support the empty space
born in Mary's eyes?

"Where could last year's snows have gone?"
asked a man who for a long time lived a calm life—or

"where have the horses of time taken Archipiada, born Thaïs?"
asked a man who for a long time lived a calm life.

Should we believe a man
who for a long time lived a calm life
but once stabbed his neighbor with a knife
and sent him too early to rest in peace?

Who will give answers to these questions?
Who will ask questions for these answers?
How long should we let it take?
How long can we feel so good!?
Could it be that it takes to be ill,
simply be ill
in order to respect the literary canon?—
just like waving a fan in cold weather,
or raising one's hands above one's head
in times of peace...

What to do!?

A Poem About Nothing

I was told by my friend,
"Everything has already been written."
So I decided to write about Nothing,
the beautiful Nothing,
Nothing that can attract you,
though I must confess
this dogmatism is by no means limited.
As I go to work and think about Nothing
my memory stops functioning
when confronting something that's full of forgetfulness,
that couldn't possibly be Nothing,
but it is!
It is so, because in the beginning there was Nothing,
and Nothing was with Nothing,
and Nothing was Nothing.
Nothing flourished in Nothing and Nothing could obtain it.
On the other hand, there is the existence of Nothing—
that has suppressed Nothing with Nothing—
we ought to remember this,
though, at the same time, there is Nothing
that Nothing cares about,
including the dichotomy.
Anyway, that's Nothing to worry about.

A poet must not forget—
to write about Nothing means Nothing from the start,
it is a Meta-Nothing, Nothing more
or less.
You can easily imagine Nothing
because it is Nothing
or even not imagining it at all
as it is Nothing.

You can imagine Nothing
and not imagining it at the same time—
because it is just Nothing.

If Nothing had not existed we should've invented it
but as there is the existence of Nothing
there's all the more reason to invent it.

Where's my Nothing!?
Who has stolen my Nothing!?
Who has cut the wings of my Nothing!?
Did a child do that?
If so, that child deserves Nothing.
Even a child knows Kako Chikobava—
once when we were drinking beer, he secretly said:
"Children have some kind of inner logic, you know,
they know perfectly well that one Nothing plus two is not three
but five of Nothing
and the antonym for both *Nothing* and *no thing* is *noting.*"
He likes puns,
and I must confess,
the puns are equally liked by children.
It is a known fact
(who knows, maybe they like Kako too...).

Anything is just as frustrating to me
as Nothing,
anything I won't explore as persistently
as Nothing.
Besides, I always had the desire to write a poem
that would have Nothing instead of an ending.
At this point I seem to be on the right way.

Porn

*Dedicated to the Ministry of Internal Affairs of Georgia, that banned
the movie* Love *by Gaspar Noé, chosing to regard it as pornography.
Also dedicated to people who publish illegal records of private life.*

Among public activities
nothing is as noble as pornography.
Sasha Grey is the single public figure
who has contributed more to the education of these generations
than Noam Chomsky, Friedrich Hegel or Dimitri Uznadze.
It's time to put porn on the curriculum
from the very first grade, teaching kids this way:
This is a violet. This is a finger, namely, the middle finger.
Teachers must appear naked at work.
Any dressed teacher would be considered reactionary,
a frigid relict of the past.
The children have the right to know the truth:
Santa Claus does not exist,
while Indigo Augustine does,
and her amazing breasts exist even more.
Confessions by Saint Indigo Augustine
seems to be apocryphal porn.
We shouldn't consider her deep throat
to be some banal eroticism.
It's the continuation of an ancient ritual,
or just a literary allusion
that brings to mind the actions of the Phallic cult.
The children should learn what their parents hide from them,
why the hands of their elder brothers tremble
when touching objects with cavities;
why their fathers show signs of desire

when the short dress of a neighborhood girl
lingers in the air like an interrogation mark.
That's why we should teach pornography in school,
better to teach Jenna Jameson and Nina Mercedez
than Friedrich Schiller, Galaktion Tabidze and Homer.
(Sasha Grey is essential to pornography, so let's get back to her later on.)
Famous intellectuals should leave place for public pornographers,
may the new generations learn!
Classes in cunnilingus will be held in ninth grade,
while final exams in BDSM are for graduates.
Any good student is sure to be whipped.
"A dildo, it's a cold iron, isn't it?" the policeman asks.
"Dildos—Prose," the young poet with a new rhyme
will shoot a round of bukkake at the ignorant policeman
(Japanese technology is always reliable!).
Some years ago Irakli Kakabadze made plans for a performance
of group-masturbation in front of the Parliament building.
But our current members of parliament did steal that idea
and perform it on a daily basis now
without defending the rights of immaterial property.
By the way, you can join them
if you still put such a deep trust in your libido.
The Porn Developing Society—
such a wonderful name for an organization
that will create an esthetic platform
for changing the basics of our ethics.
It's an oxymoron but we need to believe in it,
as Martin Luther believed in his "95 Theses,"
as Putin believes in a reunion of the Soviet Union,
as Trump believes that war can make peace,
as Bidzina Ivanishvili believes in Bidzina Ivanishvili.
There are people who walk as if
they don't touch ground at all—
and they say that porn is the perversion.
When they utter this phrase they shape their mouths
as if intending to say "O" with a grin.
One might think they weren't born after coitus

but straight out of the head of Zeus
like Pallas Athena.
Pornography is a distinguished profession,
a kind of social work,
the general discourse.
Each phallus ejaculating on Sasha Grey's face
equals a political statement,
or an important social announcement.
We must treat it seriously
and think it thoroughly through,
we must also investigate the trajectory
as it is about to set our future—
I mean by the investment of chromosomes
in various women, the penis
is like a pen writing the matrix of genes on vaginas.
You experience the mystery of porn,
the grammar of bodies,
when your *noun* penetrates her *verb*.
It couldn't be more scientific, more precise, or even clearer.
What else could a state provide?
Our country is only waiting for the ghosts of misunderstanding
when there is talk about Gaspar Noé—
although the State is against porn,
it is Love it fights, including that of Gaspar Noé,
it fights the concept of Love
as Love is not money
and won't be followed by investments.
It won't increase the budget (rather the other way around).
Oh, my God, what a crude pragmatism...
Leave us something sacred
uncorrupted by your political Darwinism.
Don't touch the innocent lagoons of RedTube, PornHub and YouPorn!
Hey, you, government officials, keep your hands off my genitalia!
Keep your hands off my hands (one is already busy).
I'll tell you a psychological fable:
Here you have the children, traumatized by porn:
the producer is ruthless:

in one of the close-ups the vagina looks directly into
the wide open eyes of the children.
A gaze so familiar and frightening, the children think,
and experience remorse.
They have yet to hear about Plato's cave story,
that's why their associations are limited to
simple feelings of fear.
As grown-ups
that gazing close-up
will always remind them of
the birth of death.

Orders

Let there be houses for the homeless,
millions for the broke,
inspiration for the poets,
a skeleton for the tongue,
sheep for the sleepless—one sheep, two sheep, three sheep...
let there be strenght for those in love
to spead themselves in each other,
let there be toys for the kids,
for the dictators too,
let there be freedom for the imagination
and food for the hungry,
let there be trees for the winds
to get some rest in the branches,

let there be nothing at all for the politicians.

Unsurviving

Even if my Lord defends the city,
the vigilance of the watchman is pointless—
nobody will survive.

Houses will be set on fire,
roads will sway,
all infants will climb out of their cradles
and kill themselves in front of people
because
nobody will survive.
The legs will start to melt on the one who is treading the long way
and a man half-buried in his own limbs
can't be saved by anyone;
snakes will flourish in our beds
and the split tongues will sprout from the walls,
and they will tell everything
that was inappropriate to talk about before.

The vigilance of a watchman,
the vigilance of mothers is pointless—
nobody will survive.

Fortune-tellers won't be able to read any palms,
readers won't be able to read any poems,
worshippers won't be able to read any prayers,
politicians won't talk so loudly,
instead they will cough and throw their bleeding tonsils away—
nobody will survive.

Plane trees will sprout leaves of cement,
passengers will lose their shadows,
words will be as heavy as stones,

our mouths will be fed up with stones
and our shadows will murmur in our place.
Nobody will survive.

All baby-sitters will abandon the babies,
with rifles carried across their shoulders they are shaped as crosses
and bless everybody in sight with a bullet
(as for the already dead, they will get their blessings
discharged just in case)—
nobody,
nobody,
nobody will survive.
Even the one likely to survive
will not survive at all,
because nobody will survive
the most severe intersection
of reason and result,
a fatal attack of
happiness and accidentality.
Nobody will survive.

It was wrong to believe
they would fathom the reasons,
provide themselves with alibis
or make arrangements.
The vigilance of the watchman is pointless,
in vain as the vigilance of cities,
meaningless as the vigilance of parents,
doing anything is like chasing the wind,
nobody,
nobody will survive.

Solution

When the sky is about to crash down,
the highly-qualified God
lowers pillars of rain
to support the leaning sky.
That's why it won't fall down on us.
That's why we always can take our chances
when it's raining.

As it is raining—we have survived...
so many times.

Alibi

We should interrogate the words,
each signification is a false alibi
covering up the blood,
the tail of crime appears at the end of the paragraph
with a blood-knitted crust.
Just pull the fossilized significations aside like a curtain
and you'll discover the word CORPSE in the word DRESSER,
or the word DOUBT embedded in the word LOVE,
or a coward in hiding behind the word FREEDOM.
The glowing syntax can no longer
agglutinate any fragments of imagination.
We should interrogate the words
meaning to be false witnesses,
covering their tracks so that we
will be eternally lost in the abyss of contractions.
Look:
The word LITTLE is bigger than the word BIG,
the black box is orange,
and LOVE... oh, what can I say...
I used to know what it meant,
but from whatever I nowadays leap
I plop down on the bottom of language.

*

I've always wanted to write bad poems,
but it demands such titanic work,
I'm forced to write only the masterpieces.

*

I'm writing
this
poem
vertically
so as to
leave
space
for
swallows'
nests.

The Schizoid Society

A Fingernail

At the threshold of night, when twilight creeps abruptly,
I've noticed my fingernails grow rapidly, at the speed of light,
at midnight they're already so long
I can easily reach the remote control
in the next room from my bed
or open the door next door and scratch the back of my neighbor,
towards the morning my thumb is erected to the sky
and touches the rising sun.
My thumb burns and I feel the pain,
as it is known to the world that the sun is red-hot.

In spite of actually being wickedly optimistic
(so optimistic that I believe in common justice,
bread becoming cheaper and the rarefaction of war),
I secretly cut my nails before full sunrise,
I don't want anybody to notice them.
I go to work as if nothing has happened.
I try to find something suspicious
but without success.
Everybody is hiding their hands
as it is known to the world
that our fingernails grow rapidly at night
and hence people can kick stars with them
or stir the clouds,
or play with the sun with a pinkie.
But in the morning all nails are cut
and we go to work,
and nobody notices anything.
As if nothing had happened,
as if no-one knew anything about long nails.

The Schizoid Society

Literature has become impossible,
as impossible as a round rectangular.
Maybe it was always like this?
Echo confirms it to me with an "Amen".
Who will make a heart out of Grammar work?
Dead poems are brought by the river.
Write as much as you want
as you can't enter one and the same poem twice.
I'm freezing so I try to import memories into poetry,
hope to keep my language warm if not my body.
I try to bring the swallows into my lines,
as well as other birds,
the girls in short skirts
as well as a couple now sitting in the park.
Why do I try to bring swallows into my lines,
or birds,
or the girls in short skirts,
or a couple now sitting in the park?
Is it possible for questions to come true?
When I write "bird" I feel its wings full of intention of flying.
Are the wings full of intention of flying when I write
that it is so after having written "bird"?
The sentences must undergo an accreditation process
before they pass the edge of any lips.
A tongue is a strict customer,
it decides to leave some sentences behind on the border.
I drink vodka to strengthen my identity—
today I am that very Paata Shamugia,
yesterday I was a fraction of that very Paata Shamugia.
I write. IwriteIwriteIwrite.
The two hemispheres of my brain are my horses,
but the left horse does not know what the right one does.

I am holding the bridles but can't keep a tight rein,
I am divided,
I am two on each side,
I am binary, feeling myself living on the minor scale,
I am writing *The Schizoid Society*.
As Pavic has mentioned in *The Dictionary of the Khazars*,
stories must, generally, be narrated twice.
So I am following that advice, endlessly repeating:
We must understand certain things,
particularly, everything.
We must understand
that poetry implies moving objects around,
and the more we insist,
the more will actually happen,
and whatever will happen is lesser than the poetry.
Poetry gives the feeling of being fed up with logistics:
Someone gives the orders: move subject A to space A1.
I am writing now. That means
every sentence inside me has been emptied,
even all possibilities of development were drained by the final agony.
The sentences are done
as soon as they have reached the climax of expression.
They resemble now the stiff showpieces in an exhibition—
let's look at "Love" (it's all covered in dust)
or "I love you," said—as a rule—in confidence and privacy...
The virgin territories of consciousness have already been ploughed,
the husband of reality—a human being—
is deprived of his right to be the first one,
this has been delegated to commercial announcements.
At present the commercials fuck the human consciousness:
Drink Fanta, be Santa,
the service of furniture transportation offers the extrapolation of objects
in the intelligible depths.
Oh, all these foreign words and not a single one is sensible!
Attention, please! The television is all about show and tell.
In one of the talk shows a politician took his clothes off. Such a scandal!
Scandal.

Scandal.
Criminal chronicles in the news.
Killers kill
but killers are killed as well.
The history repeats itself
about the boy from the old world, Abel killed by his own brother
(I don't mention his name intentionally
according to the presumption of innocence).
We are the descendants of technical fascism
and we kill the descendants of technical fascism.

Oh, Cyber-Mom, let us drink the milk from your iron breasts,
reconnect the once cut neuro-umbilical cord
and let us be tied again. The world is full of danger.
We—the Cyber-Theseuses, are by far weaker creatures
than our ancient replicas.
Ariadne is in Germany searching for an old man.

Cyber-Mom,
your cyber-children ought to make you sad!
They stand on the peak of civilization
killing one another as if they live in the wild.

"What is kitsch?"—A friend from Africa poses the question
seeing the grave of elephant bones in Sololaki,
and the philosopher immediately replies:
"Kitsch—is what you have when you fail to create something perfect."

What will poetry give us?
It doesn't produce happiness,
it won't multiply time and doesn't sell it.
What will poetry give us?
It doesn't perform as a bank,
it isn't an usurer.
It can only perform as itself
and doesn't even do this particularly well.
Why should poetry give us anything?

I'm going home to Nino, she lives in the suburbs.
Would've been nice if she lived in my neighborhood,
as friends generally should be close to each other.
I'm standing in the surroundings of a smelly bus,
I'm standing as if I were in a river.
The condensed smell of the city is closing in on me with an awkward look,
like a mom who unexpectedly caught a glance of her son masturbating.
We ignore each other in the bus.
Sweat is dripping on me like gun-powder.
A senior citizen comes floating—nobody is offering him a seat.
The flow of sweat has already brought two of my acquaintances here.
I am thinking about you right now.
I am writing about you.
Even when I write about others I write about you.
Even when I as a matter of principle don't write about you, I do.
When I listen to you,
the forest of ideas grows in my mind,
the crows of darkness fly towards this forest
and tag themselves on the twigs.
The crows grow...
My words grow too and nestle in the ears of strangers.
My words are as simple as the daily dirty dishes,
the daily dirty dishes are as simple as
my words. By replacing the items of the sum
I am simulating a mood change.
Thus I am fighting dullness, depression, loneliness.
I let you enter my house.
Look,
here's the hearth,
you can roast or boil a human being on it,
sliced or altogether, as you wish.
A human being is what he eats,
so, let's act like humans—
let's eat the meat of our fellow men
by giving our tender mouths a taste of it.
I have no home. This is my home:
The "Madonna" dinner set and "Madonna" by Raphael side by side—

denoting the linear development of ideas
as being done in *The Tin Drum*—
where the pictures of Hitler and Beethoven
resentfully look at each other
as we do—me and you—
when slipping off the smooth surface
of each other's imagination
we tell lies, endlessly and shamelessly;
as if love is to be practiced in loneliness,
and that it would be all right.
If it's not okay, we must agree
and blame God.
But he's an experienced demagogue
and will always have as an alibi
that he didn't exist when we were created.
This is the song coming from trees, the language of buds,
this is the pain, this is the joy.
This is a Georgian journalist,
in the depth of her heart—a writer.
This is a television commercial—25 60 60...
This is a mirror,
I never look in it.
The two hemispheres of my brain are my horses,
but the left horse does not know what the right one does.
I am holding the bridles but can't keep a tight rein,
I am divided,
I am two on each side,
I am binary, feeling myself living on the minor scale,
I am writing *The Schizoid Society*.

For you who each morning sow your thin fingers in my hair,
for you who makes the flutters ripen on my body
and pick up shudders from my spine,
like cherries,
for you I write this poem.

Syllogistic Self-Analysis

Dear Mom and Dad,
from now on I am going to be the best son ever,
I will acquire good manners
and will be faithful to common social rules.
As for my freakish behavior
(really embarrassing for others),
it will take shelter in the shadows of the past.
I will marry the pretty girl with proper background
and have no less than three kids,
and if blessed by God
we are going to have as many children as He decides
(I will no doubt assist God by having as much sex as possible),
I will start to write heartbreaking lyrical poems
instead of the ones with social satire,
I will stop joking about my own country,
considering every native country being sacred,
as well as people in all places—being wise
(it's obvious these two notions are different
although closely connected with the concrete of the collective unconscious,
connected in the way God connects
and the Devil divides. This phrase
implies a different idea as well,
but will be perceived correctly
as far as divine wisdom comes in hints and clues—
an approach ruining all expectations of correlative lovers, but anyway...).
So, I am going to make myself very handsome,
I promise to gain weight,
considering the philosophical discourse of Ghigla Tvaradze,
whereby any self-respecting man no taller than 180 centimeters
must weigh around 75 kilos,
and have good health too in order to share his biological harvest—
the children—with his native country.

Any man must be as the salt of the earth,
must be brave and courageous,
have a strong back and all teeth in place
(particularly those shown in a smile).
So, on the whole,
any self-respecting man must make himself handsome,
but I only weigh 65 kilos (what a shame!),
yes, that's all, I'm shamelessly slim, and moreover,
I have manners as clumsy as a paragraph by Balzac,
and as a matter of fact I am not handsome at all.

Alas! God knows I wanted to lead a proper life
but it seems to be impossible.

A Busy Poet

No visa is required from my language,
I obtain business contracts from verbs and nouns,
I use intermissions for interjections,
I'm a busy poet.

I lead diplomatic negotiations with binary oppositions,
I stand after a prefix—like a gentleman,
but I turn a blind eye to the past—impudent!
I check my base—I have to stand strong,
I'm a busy poet.

I practice all forms of interrelations—I'm in shape.
I rebuild the crumbled infrastructure of my body—I run.
For leisure I invest my hormones in the first girl I meet—oops!
Nothing personal, just poetry,
I'm a busy poet.

I set everyone free
from a life in the prison of ready-made answers.
It's time to be sentenced to peace!
It's time to be sentenced to love!
We deserve even worse!
Zero tolerance for petty obsessions!
I'm a busy poet.

I try to eliminate the separatism—
the separation of language (AKA the State)
and human beings (AKA human beings).
The one who speaks is always lying.
The one who writes is always
exposed by the lies he writes.

My lies are ordinary,
my poems extraordinary.
I'm a busy poet.

Why Do I Write?

I often ask myself this question
although unable to answer
and left without answers
I always write.
Thus, I write because I have no answer:
which could be the answer to this question—
an oblique stone thrown simultaneously
into the gardens of the questioner and the answerer.
Hopefully my next poem
will begin by depicting a beautiful landscape,
tottering infants in the green mall,
calmness,
complete calmness—
I will let a cute dog into the poem
for enhanced reactions
(after all, this common symbol of devotion
stimulates positive emotions),
and the poem will be doomed to be an answer,
to be as trustworthy as eyewitnesses.
I will provide poetry as evidence:
the whole poetry and nothing but the poetry.
But still, when I'm asked:
Why do I keep writing?
I fearfully stare at the humpback abyss
in between the question mark and my body.

Acathyst
Hymns

Kontakion 1 to Simon the Cananaean

This is what happened when the first human appeared.
He lived for some time and then he died.
His death was extremely ordinary, extremely common
but three days after his death he got up
(this you might have seen in movies),
he took a few steps and looked at the ceiling.
The smile appeared on his lips like a cannon
and he started on his poem.
That very poem is being written still and will be endless.
Even this verse of mine is the continuation of that poem
as every other poem in the world.
I caught a glimpse of a man
who was laughing from the bottom of His heart
as if He was carrying the smile on His shoulders,
a smile like a cross,
and He was followed by His co-smilers
who stood surrounded by smile
searching for the ford that they could not find.
Only He managed to cross the smile.
This is also a poem about smile—
vast and classic, an ordinary smile.
Thanks be to God.

Ikos 1 to Simon the Cananaean

Let the long year of laughter be with us,
let the buds and asphalt burst from laughter,
let the breasts of women become heavier
and half their hair turn into birds.
And every morning thereafter let them comb the nightingales,
the blackbirds,
the quails,
the hummingbirds
and peafowls,
then hunters will enter their hair
hanging on the braids.
They will shoot and kill the nightingales,
the blackbirds,
the quails,
the hummingbirds
and peafowls...
Whereby not only spring is implied
but something beyond the spring.
Thanks be to God.

Kontakion 2 to Andrew

It ain't easy
to enable spring to come,
especially when
spring is already here.
Thanks be to God.
Ain't easy either
for sidewalks to utter grass like a howl,
or for you to be lying, let's say, under an apple tree
when Sir Isaac Newton falls down on you—
it helps to sprout new ideas,
and creates the new shelter of possibilities
that is an upside down perspective of the Universe.
Thanks be to God.
It ain't easy
to shout "Eureka"
at the moment the sun is looking
straight into your eyes as a young optometrist.
This pattern of parallelism seems stupid
but, anyway, is somehow appreciated
as in reality we are mainly relativists.
Thanks be to God.
It ain't easy to enable 2 times 2 to be 4,
to have the sun held high above,
respectively, to deal with things—the truly measurable ones,
nanometers, for instance, or Aristotle's "Poetics," or Love.
Thanks be to God.
It ain't easy to be strong enough for a positive approach,
to have wide open chakras,
get a smile on the face like pimples
when going out.
Thanks be to God.
Who enabled you to read Bataille,

Debord,
Erofeev,
Anaximenes,
Pindaros,
Diadokhos,
Kldiashvili,
Samosatel,
Brautigan.
Tacit,
Shelley,
Shamugia,
Jung and Kung and fuck them all! Who knows what else...
But it ain't easy to let the Universe be all the same the whole time.
Thanks be to God.
It makes no difference if you read *Anna Karenina*
or the menu at a restaurant,
the order of things will never change.
Thanks be to God.

Ikos 2 to Andrew

There are two things that fascinate my soul.
Namely the Soviet lampshade above me and the appendix inside me.
Thanks be to God.
Someone will come and say: "There is no time for that,
reality is linear,
and won't leave any layers up for discussion."
The one saying that
will aim his eyes at me as a gun.
In the fragile routine
the monsters of everyday life sleep.
They can, it seems, recall death
by unconscious movement.
Look, as a grown-up your lovely son
will turn into a gangster or a killer,
or even worse—will be a poet—
the one combining
the eternal and the variable,
the shallow and the profound,
the ethical and the Gothic,
the Epicurean and the logical,
the comical and the mystical,
the lyrical and the practical,
the arctic and the tropic,
the technical and the immanent.
He will stand at the end of the row of winds
and have to say farewell to his insane soul
while awaiting a change in the Universe.
Thanks be to God.
Everybody or everything has a word to share on death.
This will be the word of honor.
Thanks be to God.

Kontakion 3 to James (Son of Z.)

62

Long ago, Death was considered only as death and nothing more.
Now everybody knows that Death is just a metaphor and nothing more.
It is the morphological hydra
attached to poisonous philology.
Teachers explain life with the help of death.
Their ignorance is endless.
Thanks be to God.

Ikos 3 to James (Son of Z.)

Able to be mesmerizing,
able to be mesmerized
wearing before-death-shivers
like a safety belt.
Thanks be to God.
Fighting loneliness with vodka and wine,
whisky, brandy, mulled wine, cocktails,
fight with vermouth, absinthe,
bourbon, liqueur, tequila,
and with rum in the end (all roads lead to Rome).
Thanks be to God.
Routines becoming heavier to stand, eyes becoming heavier too,
and eyelashes becoming hedgehogs,
and hedgehogs running into your eyeballs.
Thanks be to God.
As you are singing a song of the impossibility of life,
you scream like an owl
until the bloody tonsils come out of your mouth along with the sound.
Thanks be to God.
The spring outside,
the smell of flowers landing in the room
as an awkward joke.
The laughter of lovers is heard
while you are locked inside and the neighbors think you're mad.
Thanks be to God
As we know, loneliness provokes imagination and facilitates
the reproduction of forgotten content.
That's essential in an era of the insanest communications.
Thanks be to God.
And if not,
we still have to find time for comparing things.
That's easier.

Philosophy provides chronological crevices
for the gaps.
Thanks be to God.
But philosophy can't give any answers.
Thanks be to God.
Neither poetry nor math can give answers.
Thanks be to God.
Neither Web programming nor Love
can give answers.
Thanks be to God.

Kontakion 4 to Thomas

Trying to jump off the high-rise
bringing Gorgone, the jellyfish of uncertainty,
to smash it against the asphalt.
At the same time fearing the intended jump.
Having time to give threefold thanks to God and then some.
Let others die instead of you,
really, it will be more convenient.
Thanks be to God.
Let children die in wars and far from wars,
let friends and neighbors die, brothers and sisters die,
may everybody die.
Those who have leaned the hissing of the winds
against the silence that had settled between us;
And those who have opened our shadows
and pushed the southern winds into them.
Let your stupid tutors die, let enemies and friends die,
leaving you alone.
Thanks be to God.

Ikos 4 to Thomas

Theosophy has confirmed it, God does not exist,
thanks be to God.
And why not? God has the right not to exist,
a quite democratic idea.
Thanks be to God.
If I did want God to exist, however,
I would have liked Him to be portable:
folding Him you could pray, opening Him—you would chat.
If necessary you could even sit on Him—
as we know, God exists in order to give us relief, right?
Thanks be to God.
Nobody knows what kind of perspectives are hidden
in the caves of the future.
After hundreds of years, I think,
all low-esteemed third-graders
will have the power to give breath to the deceased—
this is how the future is being explained:
everything in order—
hence, unbearable.
Thanks be to God.
Human hair and nails
grow even after death.

Every particle reveals the character of the entire whole.
Immortality is possible,
thanks be to God.
I don't know who God is,
but you can see Him in my breath.
Thanks be to God.
I am sure God will deny the classical format
of representation
and during the second coming it's quite possible for Him

to appear in a limousine,
like Robert De Niro or Lady Gaga.
Thanks be to God.
That would aestheticize
the apocalypse.
To say the truth, eschatological passages always lack
a sense of esthetics.
Thanks be to God.
Esthetics are pure pleasure.
Pleasures are vulnerable.
Vulnerable things are rotten.
Rotten things die easily
in order to come back to life
and make lovers of metempsychosis dance eagerly,
dance with joy for the repeated death.
Thanks be to God.

Kontakion 5 to James (Son of A.)

Looking down the street as if it were a battlefield,
beyond which you have to lead your gaze, to spread your thoughts
focusing on a beautiful girl
who with her thighs attracts gazes and lust by the thousands.
Thanks be to God.
Her dress is mega-short above the knees,
to be precise, from below her dress is ultra-short.
["There must be some inner links among
the thought, the word and the external
object" (go to Swami Vivekananda for further information).]
Rounded butts, *mmmmm*... Round tits...
At a certain moment you can't wait any longer,
so, rushing to the bathroom aroused, you zip down your pants.
According to an old story
there is a time to collect
and a time to ejaculate.
Thanks be to God.

Ikos 5 to James (Son of A.)

Let the sun shine high in the sky
and the angry cat of hunger
run inside the stomach
scratching all intestines.
Thanks be to God.
As soon as a word like "food" is said,
the feast will suddenly appear.
This fantasy is fully realistic
as the food is really delicious.
Thanks be to God.
Who can express your joy of
teeth in motion like trooping soldiers
ramming the victims?
Possibly some beef,
beef—from a heifer called "Marianna"—
who was carrying her udder like a flag!)
Thanks be to God.

Imaginative Kontakion 6 to Judas

Sitting around the table flooded with food. Having a feast.
(By the way, culinary ontology is a separate field of study.)
Oooh, roast ox, oooh, kebab, bacon, ham, ooohham,
oooh, meat paste, pig tongue, a thousand times "OOOH,"
fresh pork sirloin steak, oooh, steak, oooh my God,
bioethics don't allow me to spread my imagination endlessly.
Oooh, bioethics! Oooh, ghomi, oooh, elarji,
oooh, chicken ragu in a clay pot, oooh, dried beans in a clay pot,
oooh, aww, pelmeni in a clay pot.
From a psychoanalytical point of view, a clay pot is the vagina
of all mothers, where pre-embryo memories whirl.
To sip soup from a clay pot is cunnilingus performed
with the aroma of incest.
Praise the aromas! Oooh, vazis tolma—the meat rolls in vine leaves!
Oooh, khinkali from Khevi—
cooked by the chef himself. Khinkali goes well
with chacha from the region of Racha...
Just imagine for a while, the trajectory of juices
from the khinkali to your arms, entwined with the flavors.
Following that very trajectory, of course,
you cannot reach a mathematical constant, oooh,
but it's possible for sure to get constant pleasure, oooh—oooh—oooh,
the pleasure.
Thanks be to God.
Oooh, my God,
threefold praises you deserve,
praised through the steaks, for God!

Imaginative Ikos 6 to Judas

The self-diagnosis is another solution:
amphetamine and methamphetamine
you can take twice a day.
Thanks be to God.
Diazepam and tizertsin three times a day.
Threefold thanks be to God.
Contraindication:
acute angle-closure glaucoma
thanks be to God.
Parkinson
thanks be to God.
Multiple sclerosis
thanks be to God.
Myasthenia
thanks be to God.
Hemiplegia
thanks be to God.
Hypotension,
hyphemia,
porphyria—
thanks be to God.

Kontakion 7 to Matthew

I used to flee,
I have escaped all potential happiness,
thanks be to God.
In all my verses
I've proved
poetry may seem to be rubbish
if
it isn't slightly more exact than math.
Thanks be to God.
When not dangerous
love is dangerous.
When not painful
exercise is useless,
when not painful it's merely
a conveyer of useless illusions.
Help raise suspicion inside you!
That's the only way to fathom the faith.
Thanks be to God.

Ikos 7 to Matthew

This is the crisis, my friends,
a big crisis of art and life.
All meaning has left us, humans.
What can we do?—we were meaningless to start with.
That's too much.
Thanks be to God.
All words and concepts resemble tasteless pedigree,
or philosophical swill.
Slurp, old bastards,
here you are, fucking bitches!
Thanks be to God.

Kontakion 8 to Peter

Hating politics as if it were hell—is the educational methadone,
continually replacing ritual with the civic Eucharist.
Seems like rejecting is
unavoidably ritual as well.
So let's say thanks to God.
Rejecting and being rejected,
a rejection of everybody
drifting like plankton in the ideological cocktail,
catching bacteria in muddy waters, then
spreading it on to others just because they are others.
A cock—screaming like the Jericho trumpet (already for the third time),
and you—connecting suspicious and unsuspicious things.
Rejecting and being rejected.
Thanks be to God.
Let all your words be bullets, unaddressed,
the shells of metabasis
by the help of which the motion changes tracks
and becomes sporadic—that's the choice,
or the white line marked in the severe marathon of existence.
Eyelashes as the swing of death,
moving on the edge of something huge and crazy.
Thanks be to God.
To be chased after and to do the chasing
is some sort of social sex,
the perversion equipped with ideological instruments.
Thanks be to God.
And rushing through the streets,
and taking each others' hearts,
and waving the hearts like flags.
Thanks be to God.

And let your blood turn into a tsunami,
and let cities be emptied and let the citizens,
frightened, step in red streams of blood,
and let this be the compensation for a rejection.
Thanks be to God.

Ikos 8 to Peter

Let your mind be purified by blood
and dedicate the rest, the rags of it,
to one whose glory was revealed on mount Tabor.
The log of all mercy and... and.... and so on.
Thanks be to God.
Sacrificing each moment to Him, being kind,
being kind in the morning
and being kind at noon,
in the market, at home, in the bathroom,
everywhere, even with foreign guests,
or while watching Japanese porn.
Wherein the girl is being raped with a toilet brush.
Thanks be to God.
Do acts of kindness
while reading *tankas*,
do uninterrupted acts of kindness.
Thanks be to God.
Kindness is the most reliable business,
no one dares to impose VAT on it.
Thanks be to God.
But it may happen that they bill it for self-interest.
I will not interfere, let them take it as they wish.
Love is a self-interest,
hate is selfish too.
It is a self-interest to walk through the plane tree ally,
as well as saying, "Do you know, my fluffy dear,
you have the prettiest eyes, and I can see myself being drowned in them."

If you wish you could be God—it could also be called a self-interest,
if you wish not to be a God, it is the same, the same self-interest.
Thanks be to God.

Kontakion 9 to John

The means of communication are ruined.
Words are left without meaning.
That's why old people complain about
the impossibility of communicating
with their physiognomy from the Mesozoic era,
with their transgression that is hidden among their wrinkles.
Oh, these silly hags and geezers.
Oh, my Lord,
why don't you kill them!?
Thanks be to God,
we don't talk about enhanced theories,
but matters that
nobody understands.
We talk about the fact that our thoughts
will never land in the appropriate ears—
this is the sign of a tragic era.
Thanks be to God.

Ikos 9 to John

At dusk the whole city diligently starts its involvement
in the neat routine of reproduction.
In short: an epidemic of screwing.
Thanks be to God.
As it happens you come out from church taking a last cigarette
whispering to the first girl you meet by chance:
"Open your mouth—
lips as fresh as a sweetly layered Baklava,
as holy as any trade secret.
Look at our breasts—they go perfectly with each other—
the coexistence of protuberances and concavities.
Thanks be to God.
If going down, aah, it's possible
to reach even a gnostic dualism,
aaah with God,
thanks be to God.
Do you really mean it? That's nothing, just forget about it.
To say the truth, that very thing
does actually mean everything,"—you answer—
"that is its majesty—a prolific life
that follows the vibrations of earth in its motion,
it's as fast as a bullet
and ruthless like the same bullet.
Thanks be to God.
Do you like Tarantino? It's a pity!
Then I will have to base my
statement on discussions only.
Thanks be to God.
Even praising a 'thing' that has numerous definitions in all languages
is interesting, mainly from the point of view of ethnic psychology,
if nothing else."
(Khhhhkh!—here you must clear your throat).

"At least we should say thanks to God.
So, thanks be to God.
Yes, there are thousands of names for it, such as:
bone,
nob,
bishop,
wang,
thang,
dong,
dagger,
banana,
cucumber,
dick (which even Sulkhan-Saba has explained in his *Bunch of Words*
as the organ of man),
Yes, let add to the list the word 'organ' as well.
Thanks be to God.
Sausage,
prick,
pecker,
wee-wee,
joystick,
log,
pole,
mustang,
meatstick,
hot dog (oh, my God, the perversion of this!)
Thanks be to God.
Let's remember the mythology:
The death of Osiris:
At the death of the powerful god Osiris,
his body was cut into 14 pieces
and buried in different places all over Egypt.
His wife Isis found all the pieces and put Osiris back together—
except for the penis,
as it had been swallowed by a fish when thrown into the Nile.
(Oh, that depraved fish!)
Thanks be to God.

But Isis had contracted for a wooden penis
and thus substituted the lost organ (e. g. bone, nob, wang,
thang, dong, prick, joystick, pole, meatstick)
of her beloved husband.
Thanks be to God.
So, from that myth it can be concluded—
Isis owned the world's first vibrator.
Thanks be to God.
Does this 'world' include Georgia? Yes, it does.
Thank God, we haven't experienced
any shortage of Mustangs in Georgia, there were quite a lot.
One of them is even displayed in a museum
as a sign of its old fame.
Thanks be to God.
As for the old Romans... excuse me, am I not tiring you with all this chat?
Thanks be to God.
As for the old Romans, they wore hand-made phalluses
around their necks to be protected from evil.
Ugh, damn!
Thanks be to God.
And here's my pussynus cuntunus—
forever ready like a hot-blooded pioneer.
Salute, comrade, hey, girl,
we are going to have fun tonight.
Thanks be to God."

Kontakion 11 by Bartholomew

When you become a pop-star your poems will be essential
and journalists swirl like mosquitos outside your house:
journalists from BBC,
from CNN,
AL-JAZIRA,
RUSTAVI 2 and CAUCASUS
(even from NATIONAL GEOGRAPHIC, to my surprise).
Journalists are trying to get exclusive mumbles out of you,
thanks be to God.
And you: laughing,
you laughinglaughinglaughing with a Homeric laughter
(during major tragedies laughter is generally the only way out),
and nobody knows about your laughter.
What do we actually know about our own laughter?
Sometimes we can hardly find it,
naturally, it doesn't mean that it doesn't exist,
at the same time, to tell the truth, neither asserts it.
Thanks be to God.

Ikos 11 by Bartholomew

82

By repeating the words indefinitely,
we can easily forget them all.
Poetry does the same—
words are killed
and their reverberations remain
in the dim mirror of routine—
thus only their dangerous, ontological substance is present.
Keep your finger moving
and leave the word—
ephemeral, inappropriate and rude
like death,
like the reproduction of Picasso's painting in TBC Bank,
like the daily tautology of birth and death.
Thanks be to God.

Kontakion 12 to Philip

And when a word reaches the ultimate depth of its representation
the world will be emptied of meaning
and insanity will rise.
Wherein the one word will float,
denote, explain and trim down everything.
Let's call that word a God,
then the sky will be a God,
then the sun will be a God,
then TIME will be a God,
I LOVE YOU will be a God,
"'TOM!' ...NO ANSWER."—will be a God,
WHAT TIME IS IT?—will be a God.
GOD IS DEAD—will be a God,
GOD will be a God.
And then
God's laughter will be spread
all over the earth.
It will set upon cities and sidewalks,
cellars will be inundated; streets will be inundated,
there will be a great flood of laughter.
I'd call it
the Guffaw Flood,
the Whoopee Flood
even the Heehaw Flood,
perhaps the Belly Laugh Flood as well.
Thanks be to God.
While the water keeps rising, traffic will be delayed,
jams and penetrating sirens howling,
and like thousands of Noah's Arks the cars
will come sailing through the Laughter Lanes and
everyone will have to stop.
And then thousands of Noahs

will climb out of their Chevrolets at the red light,
in thousands they will roll up the legs of their muddy trousers,
as one they will enter the centre of laughter—
because so it has been written.
It has been written that everything will return
to its proper source, home or lap:
the cow to its barn, the labium to the labia,
Bingo to Bongo, the worm to the womb, the womb to the woman,
the woman to the weenie, and etcetera etcetera etcetera...
Thanks be to God.
And the Almighty Mother will come.
She will come from the almighty midnight.
Her huge vagina will open like cabbage
dragging you with Her almighty partly-divine hands and
pushing you back to where you came from.
You will be resisting with
your sneakers sliding on the labia majora
and at the end you will surrender,
because so it has been written (as I've already mentioned above):
everything will return to its origin,
everything repeats itself
taking nothing into consideration.
Thanks be to God.

Ikos 12 to Philip

Let's reveal the truth—
God is nothing but a devil with an inferiority complex,
who admitted His son to die on a cross.
Thanks be to God.
In His youth maybe
the cherubs didn't want to fuck Him,
maybe that's why He himself has invented His self
as being the center of the Universe, the creator.
Thanks be to God.
Maybe He suffered from some kind of disease,
maybe He was dystrophic
or had bronchospasms too often.
Thanks be to God.

Why was there an apple tree in Eden?
Maybe the God needed more vitamin C?
Maybe He was beaten by the stronger boys in His childhood?

Of course, I do realize the coexistence of
the unambiguity of my ideas
and my artistic atheism.
Thanks be to God.
All the same, I know, of course,
that no religion can lead beyond the point of Atheism,
though, as Boris Gross declared,
we happen to live now in the age of the departed Protestantism.
So, most importantly we have to endure.
And why not? We do endure, we will endure.
Thanks be to God.

Anonymous Kontakion 13

I can hear Your name, my God,
Thou, who have transformed clouds into rain
and let us feel the dewdrops.
Thou who created the Universe wasting, as we all know, all Your efforts,
and Thou who were in the beginning,
let me be precise, Thou were the first, before everything appeared.
Thou have exposed a storm like a lullaby
and we passed through that lullaby,
we—who were tired and disgusting,
fearless,
hoping You are here, my God,
Thou who have suppressed laughter with laughter
and opened the gate of the hell with Your foot
and pushed the sinners kicking to paradise
(don't hesitate, they have deserved it!).
Thou who have airdropped the holy spirit into our vulnerable bodies
and thus have alleviated the load of vanity on us,
thou who have opened Your body as if You had a zipper
and put Your eyelashes between the being and the non-being,
like the immortal Pont Mirabeau,
immortalized thanks to Apollinaire.
As for the bridge itself, it is no masterpiece at all.
Thou who have woven my dreams from autumn grass
and from the songs of the nightingale;
Thou who have created both genders in bed, and death in Somalia,
moreover taking it easy, Thou have admitted a massacre of children.
Thanks for having granted us soil under our feet and screams in our ears
along with words from the televised presidential speech,
along with banned phrases from disappointed madmen,
along with exasperated memories about mom,
along with handmade dreams
quite offensively and rudely stripped of ornaments,

Thou who have raised our tears to the skies
to hang our night shudders on stars,
to plant our everyday smiles in space
like banners.
Indeed,
that's one small smile for man, one giant laugh for mankind!
We are all grateful to You,
it could not be otherwise.
Thanks be to God.

Anonymous Ikos 13

Who has opened our dreams?
Who has sowed severe vigilance
in the crevices of dreams?
Who has raised our shadows on the sidewalks?
Who has sowed death around the corners?
Who has scratched wrinkles on my mother's forehead?
Who causes death?
What is the ultimate point of death but forgetfulness?
Who has put those flowers miserably on my tombstone?
—Will it help us to feel erected?, I ask
—It will really help you to feel elevated!, God answers.
—Sit down, God! You have not performed with excellence today.
You don't understand anything at all,
nothing at all in the world!
You are in the skies on Your own
and You feel at peace
while the statistics yell:
15 million children die of hunger every year,
every 25th person in the world suffers from chronic hunger,
thereamong—16 million children under the age of 5,
natural disasters have killed 295.000 people,
at this moment 3 billion people strive just to stay alive.
Yesterday a mom killed her child.
the day before yesterday it was the other way around,
anyway, we are thankful,
thanks be to God
thanks so on
and so on.

Advantage

Hero

Utilize the power (vibrant in muscles)
to make things happen,
hang your anger on the tail of winds.
Be flexible towards the dream,
be fragile and awkward towards reality.
Sow drought in the throat, already ripen,
and reap the water, the wine, the Coke,
whatever you reach, as long as it's liquid.
Let your knee-caps travel
from bed to bed,
forge the dream,
become a hero!

Compromise

I believe I saw God
standing in front of the post office
holding my book and a bottle
of vodka. I believe this makes no
sense and that the order of things
is unchanged. I believe
poetry will become crime stories
and at the end of the news
the anchors will rhyme a bank robbery
and a crime of passion
or Justin Bieber's suspicious
behavior (and even more suspicious
career) and a weather report, which
will be as aesthetic as bucolic
poetry. I believe love
sometimes really exists
like when your kiss turns
my body into booty. I believe
that in our time acting evil's boring
and only depressed bankers
practice it. I believe that a person
can die several times in a day
with no hope of being reborn—
which is not honorable behavior.

I believe that death is a shameful
compromise and that's why I don't
believe in those who manage it.

Trading Places

Hey, God, let's trade places!
You be Paata Shamugia
and I'll be God.
It's not as hard as it looks.
Lose some weight, let
your hair grow out, start
chain smoking. It'll be a
bit boring, but by God you'll
play it smart (just don't
put me in any hot water)!

Every morning, you'll wake up
in the studio and start getting calls
from your temporary father
(my old dad) about your uselessness.
You'll get used to it.

I'll be with the angels, taking on
Godlike manners, looking at earth
through the ozone. And every time
I want to change something, I
can change something. Finally.
I'll feel like that.

Contra Epos

Trajectory

I am my own friend.
I live a hundred miles away from me,
a hundred tears,
a hundred dreams.
I am my own brother.
Buses run between me and myself and
I am my own father
and the passing buses leave behind fumes and sorrows.
It's so cold at night I am lazy to think of high values
and I am my own friend who is
freezing and feels lazy and is full of fear
and I am my own friend.
If I die
(I can't deny it will happen some day)
no president will come to my funeral,
so there won't be any speeches full of historical stupidity,
neither will there be any new Marilyn Manson
to sing me a post-satanic hallelujah.
And the revered citizen Zurab Tsereteli
won't erect a golden statue of me in
the Freedom Square of Tbilisi,

I am just my own friend...

The You-Centrist

It's going to rain tomorrow so cars will move slowly,
no beautiful girls will come out on their balconies
and the lovely couple walking in the rain without umbrella
will take shelter in each others bodies instead.
This will be because I love you.

There was a soldier from Costa Rica, who smiled
to the embarrassed journalist, telling her
it is better to eat grass while standing
than to eat beefsteaks kneeling down,
though it couldn't change anything in the universe.
This will be because I love you.

A sunny day will come the day after tomorrow
and sidewalks will sprout people.
The kid from the car accident will
unexpectedly, and fortunately of course, recover.
This will be because I love you.

Some day there won't be (and never again)
any wars and atomic bombings
and the language of love will be accessible to everybody.
Then that neighborhood couple will come out on their balcony
with their two lovely crying baby-angels in diapers,
and everybody will feel happy
including me and everyone within me,
everyone I represent right now.
And this will be because I love you.

Philosophers have agreed on the essence of life,
which is, to say the truth, very unclear—
so that everybody can understand it.

At nights a very poor poet is writing his poems
while the neighbors gossip about a slut by the name of Gulnara.
I'm not able to change anything,
so I just smoke and walk slowly through the darkness of midnight
saying to the first one I encounter, that I love her.

A Television Commercial

Yearning for home.
Yearning for tea.
Yearning for coffee.
Yearning for sex.
Yearning for sex in Cleopatra's bathroom.
Yearning for a television commercial.
Yearning for the second volume of psychoanalysis by Sigmund Freud,
and the third volume of psychoanalysis by Sigmund Freud,
and the fourth volume of psychoanalysis by Sigmund Freud.
I need evolution.
I need psychological mutation.
I need for me to be Walt Whitman
and for you to be terrorists.
Need Dada.
Need Daddy.
Need the EU and the EU standards in repair works.
Yearning for fizzlings,
for fine fieldfares,
for Fred and the fortress,
for *It's Far to Gurjistan*
for a furious man with black fur hat.
I need black asphalt.
I need Linda.
I need pandas.
Yearning for inclusive angels
and exclusive BBC programs.
Need to have 100 million on my private bank account
and an appointed private meeting with Miss USA.
I need coffee.
I need coffee,
a cup of coffee on wasteland islands.
Yearning for asymmetrical gods

and symmetrical friendship.
I need to know the formula for economical collapses
and for human happiness too.
I need cheap vodka
and a yacht in the Pacific.
I need The Goncourt Prize and after that
I need The Booker Prize and after that
I need The Nobel Prize as well.
I need prizes to buy a house,
to buy dolls for my wife,
to buy myself a tranquil death,
to buy a small piece of land in Paradise
where I could oversleep.

*

Nothing will change. Everything will come back.
Flying dreams will set upon our sleep
to sing of the past and the sidewalks.
Winds will have their hair combed by antennas,
killers will weep by the bodies of their victims
but nothing will change.
We will experience more and more of wars and tears,
hatred and suicide,
we will dance in the shadows of our own bodies,
we will dance in the shadows of the suppressed poets,
we will dance we will dance we will dance we will dance
and nothing will change.
Everything will come back.

A new morning will come again. And you will envy
your friend for marrying a masterpiece.
What about you? You waste your time,
lose all your friends. You've lost your dad, even your mom,
and faith as well. And by that you are losing your right
to be dead.
And there is your right not to hear your dad scorning you
for jobs not taken, for being out of wedlock,
not having received the Nobel Prize...
See? As I said before,
nothing will change...

Notes

"Literature and Technology"
Lasha Nadareishvili—Poet, and editor of "Asaval-dasavali," the main Georgian nationalistic newspaper.

"The Interrogative Sentence"
Where could last year's snows have gone?—A line from "Ballad of Ladies of Yore" by French poet François Villon.
where have the horses of time…—Shamugia is paraphrasing the theme of the Villon poem.

"A Poem About Nothing"
Kako Chikobava—A Georgian leftist poet.

"Porn"
Irakli Kakabadze—Contemporary Georgian writer and performer.
Bidzina Ivanishvili—Former prime minister of Georgia.

"The Schizoid Society"
Sololaki—An old part of Tbilisi.
The Tin Drum—A novel by Günter Grass.

"Syllogistic Self-Analysis"
Ghigla Tvaradze—A neighbor of the poet.

"Acathyst Hymns"
Acathyst Hymns—The Acathyst Hymn, usually recited by Eastern Orthodox or Eastern Catholic Christians, is dedicated to a saint, holy event, or one of the entities of the Holy Trinity. Its significance for religious worship is evident, as only during readings of the Gospel and when Acathyst Hymns are being sung, it is considered mandatory for the congregation to stand up.

"Kontakion 3 to James (Son of Z.)"
James (Son of Z.)—I.e. James, son of Zebedee.

"Kontakion 5 to James (Son of A.)"
James (Son of A.)—I.e. James, son of Alphaeus.

"Imaginative Kontakion 6 to Judas"
ghomi... elarji... pelmeni... vazis tolma...—Traditional Georgian dishes.
Khinkali—Georgian meat dumplings with broth inside.
Chacha—Georgian vodka, normally made on grapes.
Racha—A mountainous part of West Georgia

"Ikos 9 to John"
bone, nob, bishop...—The words for penis relate to the storyline in "The
Man from Hollywood," Quentin Tarantino's segment of the film *Four
Rooms*.
Sulkhan-Saba—Prince Sulkhan-Saba Orbeliani (1658-1725), a Georgian
writer and diplomat.

"Kontakion 12 to Philip"
'TOM!'...NO ANSWER.—The first lines of *The Adventures of Tom Sawyer*
by Mark Twain

"A Television Commercial"
It's Far to Gurjistan—A Georgian documentary from 1970, about Geor-
gians living in Iran.